☆ ☆ ☆

George Bush

George Bush

Betsy Ochester

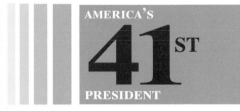

AMERICA'S

41ST

PRESIDENT

Children's Press®
A Division of Scholastic Inc.
New York / Toronto / London / Auckland / Sydney
Mexico City / New Delhi / Hong Kong
Danbury, Connecticut

Library of Congress Cataloging-in-Publication Data

Ochester, Betsy.
    George Bush / Betsy Ochester.
        p. cm. — (Encyclopedia of presidents. Second series)
    Includes bibliographical references and index.
    ISBN 0-516-22971-0
    1. Bush, George, 1924– 1. Juvenile literature. 2. Presidents—United
States—Biography—Juvenile literature. I. Title. II. Encyclopedia of presidents
(2003)
E882.O28'2005
973.928'092—dc22   2004022028

CHILDREN'S PRESS and associated logos are trademarks and or registered
trademarks of Scholastic Library Publishing. SCHOLASTIC and associated
logos are trademarks and or registered trademarks of Scholastic Inc.
1 2 3 4 5 6 7 8 9 10 R 14 13 12 11 10 09 08 07 06 05

Contents

Chapter 1

Shot Down

Early on the morning of September 2, 1944, a squadron of U.S. Navy dive-bombers soared over the Pacific Ocean toward their target—a radio tower used by the enemy Japanese on the island of Chichi-Jima. One plane was piloted by George Bush, one of the youngest pilots in the navy. As Bush pushed his plane into an attack dive, Japanese anti-aircraft fire blasted around him. "The flak was the heaviest I'd ever flown into," he said later.

Suddenly, a powerful jolt rocked the plane up and forward, "as if a massive fist had crunched into the belly of the plane," Bush recalled. "Smoke poured into the cockpit, and I could see flames rippling across the crease of the wing, edging toward the fuel tanks."

Still, Bush pressed on toward his target and dropped his four 500-pound (225-kilogram) bombs. Then he headed back out to sea.

7

Twenty-year-old U.S. Navy pilot George Bush in the cockpit of his World War II plane in 1944.

The smoke in the cockpit began to choke him. When he could see the ocean below, Bush called out to his two crewmen, ordering them to bail out. The plane was going down.

As Bush ejected from the plane, he suffered a nasty gash on his forehead, but his parachute opened, and he floated down to the open sea. He reached his life raft, inflated it, and got in. A pilot from his squadron spotted him, but so did the Japanese, who sent out ships to capture him. Bush kept hoping to catch sight of his two crewmen, but sadly, neither he nor his squadron found any trace of them.

Two hours went by. Suddenly, only 100 yards (90 meters) away, a small black dot was rising from the water. It was a periscope. A submarine was surfacing. Was it Japanese or American? He was relieved to learn that it was a U.S. sub, the *Finback*. Sailors threw him a line and pulled his raft close, then helped him clamber aboard. "Let's get below," a crew member said. "The skipper wants to get out of here." Soon the *Finback* disappeared again beneath the water's surface.

Bush knew how lucky he was. He could have been knocked unconscious by the antiaircraft fire and gone down with his plane. He could have drowned before any rescuers arrived. Or he might have been captured and subjected to harsh treatment by the Japanese. Yet he had survived to fight another day. More than 50 years later, Bush said, "I put my experience as a 'combat Navy flier' right up at the top of the list of experiences that truly shaped my life. . . . I went in a kid. I emerged a man."

Family Values ———————————————————

The navy pilot—and future president of the United States—grew up in a close-knit loving family in a world of comfort and privilege. George Herbert Walker Bush was born on June 12, 1924, in Milton, Massachusetts, the second of five children. He was named for his grandfather, George Herbert Walker, who was always called "Pop" by his family. Young George quickly became known as "Poppy" or "Little Pop." The nickname stuck through his childhood and into his adult years.

When Poppy was a year old, his family moved to Greenwich, Connecticut, a wealthy suburb of New York City. From the time he was seven, they lived in a large house on Grove Lane, with eight bedrooms and a wide, spacious porch. The grounds offered plenty of space for George and his siblings, Prescott Jr., Nancy, Jonathan, and William (Bucky) to play. In addition to the Bush family, the household included a cook, a maid, and a gardener.

Prescott and Dorothy Bush were used to wealth and comfort, but they did not believe in spoiling their children. They believed strongly in family, faith, and service—values George would hold dear all his life. Prescott was a partner in a

The Bush family home in Greenwich, Connecticut.

Wall Street investment bank, commuting each weekday into New York City. At breakfast, he and Dorothy read the Bible aloud, and the family attended church regularly.

"I don't think there's a man I've ever had more respect for than my own father," George said years later. Prescott had high expectations for his children. He impressed on them his belief that the more advantages a young person has in life, the more will be expected of him or her.

Part of the Bush family on their front steps. From left to right: mother Dorothy Walker Bush, George, Nancy, Jonathan, and father Prescott Bush.

Dorothy Walker Bush believed in bringing up a family with "generous measures of both love and discipline." An energetic and attractive woman, she taught her children to be fair and not to gloat over winning. Both Dorothy and Prescott were gifted athletes, and sports played a big part in the Bush family's life. The Bushes taught that it was never acceptable to brag, but they played hard and enjoyed winning.

Poppy felt especially close to his older brother, Pres. Both collected matchbooks, stamps, and baseball cards. George was a generous boy, always eager to share his toys and snacks. His friends and family sometimes called him "Have Half," because he usually offered to split any special treat that he received.

Maine to Massachusetts ————————————

"We were a close, happy family," George wrote later, "and never closer or happier than when we crammed into the station wagon each summer—five kids, two dogs, with Mother driving—to visit Walker's Point in Kennebunkport, Maine." On Walker's Point, a peninsula jutting into the Atlantic Ocean, the Walker-Bush house was constantly filled with cousins, friends, and neighbors. George and Pres slept on a screened-in porch at night. During the days, the children fished, played tennis, explored tidal pools, and read. One of their favorite activities was riding with their grandfather in his lobster boat, *Tomboy*. When George was nine, he and Pres took the boat out on the Atlantic by themselves for the first time. A sudden storm came up, bringing strong winds and choppy water. Though frightened, the boys managed to bring the boat safely to shore.

During the school year, George attended the private Greenwich Country Day School. When he was 13, he left home to enroll at Phillips Academy in Andover, Massachusetts. He joined his brother Pres at the famous prep school,

George Bush at Phillips Andover, when he was 15 or 16 years old.

which made it easier to adjust to being away from home. George soon became a popular student, easily making friends and impressing teachers with his good manners and pleasant nature. In his senior year he was captain of the baseball and soccer teams, a member of the basketball team, and president of the senior class.

Love and War

On December 7, 1941, 17-year-old George Bush was walking across the Andover campus when he heard some astounding news. The Japanese had attacked Pearl Harbor in Hawaii, destroying dozens of U.S. navy ships and killing thousands of U.S. servicemen. War was already raging in Europe and Asia. Now it was clear the United States would join its allies in World War II against Japan and Germany. Like most other Americans, George reacted strongly to the sneak attack. He vowed that he would enlist in the military as soon as he turned 18.

Smoking ruins of ships at Pearl Harbor, Hawaii, after the sneak attack by Japanese warplanes on December 7, 1941.

A few weeks later, another life-changing event occurred. At a Christmas dance in Greenwich, he met a girl named Barbara Pierce. He asked her to dance, then they sat down to talk. George learned that 16-year-old Barbara was from nearby Rye, New York, and home on break from school in South Carolina. When Barbara got home that night, she gushed to her mother that she'd met the "nicest, cutest boy, named Poppy Bush." Through the rest of the school year, the young couple wrote to each other often. That spring, George asked Barbara to his senior prom at Andover.

George graduated from Andover in June 1942, only weeks before his 18th birthday. He had been accepted to Yale University, and his father urged him to go to college before enlisting for military service. George was determined, however. On his 18th birthday, he went to Boston and signed up for the navy, hoping to become a naval pilot. Soon he was in North Carolina for preflight training. He received his aviator's wings on June 9, 1943. A few days short of his 19th birthday, Bush was the youngest aviator in the navy.

In August 1943, George was home on leave. He invited Barbara to join the Bush family at Kennebunkport. During a long walk on the rocky coastline, George and Barbara secretly got engaged. Then he returned to his unit. The wedding would have to wait. He thought about Barbara often, however, and when he got his own plane, he named it after her.

Barbara Bush during her teen years.

Fast Facts

WORLD WAR II

Who: The Axis powers (Germany, Italy, and Japan) against the Allied powers (Great Britain, France, the Soviet Union, the U.S., and others)

When: September 1939 through August 1945; the United States entered the war after the Japanese attack on Pearl Harbor, Hawaii, on December 7, 1941.

Where: Europe (including the Soviet Union), Southeast Asia, North Africa, islands in the Pacific Ocean, and on the seas

Why: Germany, Italy, and Japan had invaded neighboring countries in search of territory, natural resources, and power; Allied nations went to war to end their aggression.

Outcome: Italy surrendered in 1943; Germany in May 1945 after the capture of its capital, Berlin; Japan in August 1945 after the U.S. dropped atomic bombs on two if its cities. Germany and Japan were occupied by Allied troops; the United States and the Soviet Union emerged as the two world superpowers.

One day in 1944, Barbara Pierce received a letter from a pilot in George Bush's squadron. He broke the news that George's plane had gone down, but could provide no information about George himself. The Bush family received similar reports. For days they waited to learn George's fate. Finally the navy reported that George had been rescued.

The submarine that rescued Bush was on a combat mission. Bush had to stay on board for a month as the submarine finished its patrol. He finally returned to his unit, which was now based in the Philippine Islands. During his service, George flew 58 combat missions. For the bravery in completing his mission on September 2, 1944, he was awarded the Distinguished Flying Cross.

In December 1944, George came home on leave. "No reunion could have been scripted more perfectly." he wrote. "I arrived Christmas Eve. There were tears, laughs, hugs,

George and Barbara (third and fourth from left) on their wedding day with family members.

joy, the love and warmth of a family in a holiday setting." And there was Barbara.

They were married two weeks later, on a snowy January 6 at the First Presbyterian

Church in Rye.

George was assigned to train new navy pilots, and in the next six months, he spent time in Florida, Michigan, and Maine. In August 1945, he and Barbara were living in Virginia Beach, Virginia, and George was preparing to serve another tour overseas. Then on August 14, President Harry Truman announced that Japan had agreed to surrender, ending World War II. In Virginia Beach and around the country, the streets filled with cheering crowds. Now George and Barbara were free to return to their peacetime lives.

"Much Love to All, Pop"

Some letters began "Dear Mum and Dad," others "My darling Bar." Many were filled with a playful sense of humor. George Bush's letters home from World War II marked the start of a lifelong love of correspondence. Early on, his parents taught Pop the value of sending short thank-you notes. It was a lesson he took to heart. Later as a politician, he became famous for his kind, genuine, and timely correspondence. Biographer John Robert Greene remarked, "His thank-you notes, written for what one might consider the most trivial of favors, were Washington legends." Bush remained a faithful correspondent with childhood friends, Texas buddies, and family members old and young. In addition, his notes would one day help win the support of politicians and the trust of world leaders.

☆☆☆

Yale

George and Barbara moved to New Haven, Connecticut. He joined the largest freshman class in Yale's history—some 8,000, including nearly 5,000 veterans. He received academic credits for studies that were part of his military training, allowing him to finish college in two and a half years. "Like other married veterans in the late 1940s," Bush wrote, "I was on a fast track to get my degree and make up for lost time." He and Barbara were also eager to start a family. Their first son, George Walker Bush, was born on July 6, 1946.

Even though he was taking a heavy load of courses, Bush found time to be active in campus activities. He jointed a fraternity and became a member of the prestigious secret society Skull and Bones. His favorite activity was baseball. In 1947 and 1948, Bush was the first baseman and captain of Yale baseball teams that reached the College World Series. (Yale lost the deciding game both years.) George majored in economics. Even with all his activities and his young family, he was a good student and graduated with honors.

Bush's father and his grandfather both directed prestigious banking firms in New York. George could have had a job with either one, but he did not want to ride his family's coattails to success. As he wrote, he and Barbara "wanted to make our own way, our own mistakes, and shape our own future."

Two future presidents: George H. W. Bush with George W. Bush on his shoulders in 1947.

Then Neil Mallon, an old family friend, gave George some advice. Mallon, an executive in the oil business, said, "What you need to do is head out to Texas and those oil fields. That's the place for ambitious young people these days." He offered George an entry-level job as an equipment clerk at one of his companies in Texas. "There's not much salary," Mallon said, "but if you want to learn the oil business, it's a start."

George eagerly signed on for the adventure.

Chapter 2

Hard Work ——————————————————————

West Texas in the summertime was unlike anything George Bush had ever seen. As he drove down Highway 80 toward Odessa that first day, his eyes took in the dry soil and tumbleweeds, punctuated by an occasional tree. It was quite a change from the wooded hills of New England. George quickly found an apartment and sent for Barbara and baby George. Their new home was half of a scruffy, narrow house with a shared bathroom. The thin partition that divided the apartments did little to mask the noise from the other side.

Neil Mallon had warned that Bush would start at the bottom, and he did. As an equipment clerk, he painted oil machinery in the scorching sun and swept out warehouses, but there were also chances to learn. After a year, he was promoted to salesman in California, selling oil drilling equipment. In the following months, the Bushes lived in Whittier, Bakersfield, Ventura, and Compton, California. In 1949, a daughter, Pauline Robinson Bush, was born in California. The family called her "Robin."

Bush found the constant travel and frequent moves difficult. He was pleased when the company transferred him back to Midland, Texas, in April 1950. The Bushes bought a small house in Midland, in a development nicknamed "Easter Egg Row." All the houses were the same, except for their color. The Bush family's "egg" was light blue. George and Barbara threw themselves into life in Midland, which was then a booming oil town. They hosted Sunday afternoon barbecues for neighbors, taught Sunday School, and got involved in many community activities. George coached Little League baseball.

In 1951 George and one of his neighbors, John Overbey, decided to take a gamble and start their own oil business, the Bush-Overbey Oil Development Company. The new partners worked around the clock to make a success of their new venture. George traveled more than he had as a salesman, searching for investors and landowners willing to sell oil rights. The hard work paid off. The business was a success.

In 1953, Bush and Overbey combined their operation with a firm owned by two other friends, Bill and Hugh Liedtke. The partners agreed to raise a million dollars to expand the business. Bush's family connections came in handy

George Bush asks questions of an oil worker in West Texas.

when searching for investors willing to risk their money in a start-up oil company. Next, the partners needed a name for their new venture. That problem was solved by the movie playing in Midland at the time, *Viva Zapata!*, which depicted the Mexican revolutionary Emiliano Zapata. The four partners decided that "Zapata" had just the right ring. They took some risks choosing where to drill, and their gambles paid off. By the end of 1953, Zapata was pumping more than a thousand barrels of oil a day, worth $1 million a year.

Black Gold

George Bush arrived during a booming time in the Texas oil industry. Then and now, Texas is the largest oil-producing state in the country. The American oil industry began in Pennsylvania in 1859, when oil was sold mainly as a fuel for lighting. By 1901 huge new oil deposits were discovered in east Texas. As the automobile became a familiar sight in the country, the demand for oil skyrocketed. The west Texas oil fields added to the state's oil dominance during the 1950s. During George Bush's career in the business, still another oil source was discovered—underwater oil fields in the Gulf of Mexico. Today, about one-fifth of the nation's oil production comes from the Lone Star State.

Texas oilmen soon became active overseas as well as at home. Many worked in the Middle East, which proved to have greater oil reserves than Texas itself. When George Bush became president, he led a crusade to protect oil-rich Kuwait when it was attacked by its neighbor, Iraq.

☆ ☆ ☆

Tragedy

One day in the spring of 1953, young Robin Bush woke up pale and listless. Barbara took her to the family pediatrician for a checkup. Later that day, the doctor delivered horrible news. Three-year-old Robin had advanced leukemia, a cancer of the blood. Within days, the Bushes flew to New York with Robin, where she was checked into Memorial Sloan-Kettering Hospital, famous for treating cancer. Robin was given experimental cancer-fighting drugs, and Barbara stayed in New York at her side. George commuted back and forth between Texas, helping care for George (then seven years old) and Jeb, who had

George Bush with young George and Robin in 1953. Later that year, Robin died of leukemia.

been born earlier that year. Robin remained at Sloan-Kettering for seven months. Sometimes it seemed she was getting better, but in October, she died.

George and Barbara were overcome by grief. Barbara became so distraught that she thought life wasn't worth living. She later wrote that George saved her during that dreadful period, with his faith, love, and optimism.

Bitten by the Bug

George continued to work hard at Zapata, and his family continued to grow. Two new sons, Neil and Marvin, were born. In 1959, the Bushes had another daughter, Dorothy, whose nickname was "Doro." That same year, Bush and his partners decided to divide Zapata. Bush had grown increasingly interested in offshore drilling for oil. He bought and ran Zapata Off-Shore, which used huge floating oil rigs to dig wells on the ocean floor. To be closer to the wells in the Gulf of Mexico, Bush moved his family to Houston, the largest city in the state. Bush's business instincts proved profitable. By 1964, Zapata Off-Shore was prospering—with four monster drilling rigs and 195 employees.

As the company thrived, Bush began to think about politics. His father had been elected to the U.S. Senate from Connecticut in 1952 and was just completing ten years of service. When Republican leaders in Houston asked George Bush to run for chairman of the Harris County Republican party in the spring of 1962, he didn't hesitate. "This was the challenge I'd been waiting for," Bush remembers, "an opening into politics at the ground level, where it all starts."

For the next several weeks, George and Barbara campaigned every night. The Republican party was a minority party in Texas at the time, and Bush spoke about strengthening the two-party system by enrolling more Republicans. He easily won election and set to work. His enthusiasm and energy attracted many new volunteers and recruits.

Local Republicans were supportive when Bush decided to run for the U.S. Senate in 1964. He wanted to unseat liberal Democratic senator Ralph Yarborough. With Barbara, he set out on the campaign trail, running a folksy campaign filled with barbecues, country music, and large doses of backslapping and handshaking. Barbara designed and gave away handmade straw purses, stitched with elephants and the words "Bush for Senate."

While Bush was campaigning in November of 1963, tragedy struck when President John F. Kennedy was shot and killed in Dallas. As the nation mourned, Vice President Lyndon B. Johnson became president. Johnson was a Texan and a former senator who was still powerful in the state. In 1964 Johnson ran for a full term as president against conservative Republican Barry Goldwater. Bush aligned himself with Goldwater's conservatism, changing some of his own views to try to attract voters. In a state where civil rights legislation was unpopular, Bush criticized Senator Yarborough for voting in favor of the Civil Rights Act of 1964.

A rally for Senate candidate George Bush during his 1964 campaign. He lost the election to Democrat Ralph Yarborough.

In Texas and the country as a whole, voters rallied behind President Johnson, electing him by a landslide over Goldwater. Thanks in part to Johnson's strong showing, Ralph Yarborough defeated George Bush and gained re-election to the Senate. After the loss, Bush told his minister in Houston, "I took some far-right positions to get elected. I hope I never do it again. I regret it."

Bush continued to work for Zapata, but he had become fond of politics. He wrote, "In Midland I was bitten by the bug that led me into the oil business. Now I'd been bitten by another bug." In 1966 he decided to run for a seat in the U.S. House of Representatives in a district that included part of Houston. He resigned as president of Zapata Off-Shore to devote himself fully to his campaign. His opponent was a conservative Democrat, Frank Briscoe. Bush and Briscoe were remarkably similar in their stands on the issues. Bush portrayed himself as a man who could get things done in Washington. His

Victory! George and Barbara Bush celebrate his election to the U.S. House of Representatives in 1966.

campaign posters said, "Elect George Bush to Congress and Watch the Action."

On election night, some 2,000 people packed Bush's Houston headquarters. They weren't disappointed: Bush was elected, with 57.6 percent of the vote. He was the first Republican ever to represent Houston in Congress.

Congressman Bush

As a first-year congressman, George Bush was appointed to the House Ways and Means Committee, the oldest and most powerful committee of the House. It has great influence on the federal budget and considers all tax legislation. Bush was the first freshman congressman in more than 60 years to be appointed to this

1968

George Bush's vote for the Fair Housing Act occurred in a year filled with many unexpected twists and turns. These were some of the major events:

January 31	Enemy forces in Vietnam began a powerful offensive against 100 cities and towns
March 12	Antiwar Democrat Eugene McCarthy nearly defeated President Johnson in the New Hampshire Democratic primary for president
March 30	President Johnson dropped out of presidential race to concentrate on ending the war
April 4	Civil rights leader Martin Luther King Jr. was assassinated in Memphis, Tennessee
June 5	Senator Robert Kennedy, the leading antiwar Democrat, was assassinated in Los Angeles
August 8	Republicans nominated former vice president Richard Nixon for president
August 28	The Democratic convention nominated Vice President Hubert Humphrey for president while antiwar demonstrators clashed with police outside the convention hall
November 5	Richard Nixon defeated Humphrey for the presidency, promising "peace with honor" in Vietnam and "a return to law and order" at home

☆☆☆

committee. This was the first of several surprising appointments Bush would receive in Washington.

In April 1968, Bush angered some of his conservative supporters in Texas when he voted for President Johnson's Fair Housing Act. The act aimed to stop discrimination against African Americans and other minorities when buying or renting housing. Bush received stacks of hate mail, but he defended his vote. If an applicant for a home or apartment meets all reasonable requirements, Bush said, he "should not have the door slammed just because he is a Negro, or because he speaks with a Mexican accent."

In the 1968 campaign, Democrats in Houston put up no opposition to George Bush's run for re-election to the House. This gave Bush time to campaign for Republican presidential candidate Richard Nixon. Grateful for the support, Nixon became a supporter of Bush's political career.

Two years later, in 1970, Nixon and former president Johnson both urged Bush to run against Democratic senator Ralph Yarborough once again. Bush gave up his seat in the House and stepped up to the challenge, campaigning with his usual zeal. His ads described him as "in step with the Texas of today," and claimed "he can do more."

Democrats threw Bush a curve, however. In the Democratic primaries, the liberal Yarborough was defeated by conservative Democrat Lloyd Bentsen. Most of Bentsen's views were very much like Bush's, and a majority of voters in the state were still registered as Democrats. Bentsen won the election, dealing Bush his second serious electoral defeat.

Bush was bitterly disappointed, but he tried to be positive. "It's a character builder," he said. "I think I'm a better person because I tasted defeat." His eleven-year-old daughter Dorothy didn't find defeat so easy. In tears, she said to her mother, "I'll be the only girl in the fifth grade whose Daddy doesn't have a job."

Fortunately, President Nixon appreciated Bush's strong support and offered him a big new job—one that would take the Bush family to New York City.

Chapter 3

Ambassador

President Nixon appointed George Bush the United States ambassador to the United Nations. The appointment surprised many, since Bush had no previous experience in the diplomatic world. The *New York Times* wrote, "There seems to be nothing in his record that qualifies him for this highly important position."

The criticisms just stirred Bush's sense of competition. "They laid down a challenge," he said. "I was determined to prove them wrong." It turned out that he had a natural ability for diplomacy. His ability to make friends and to gain the trust of others made him an effective ambassador.

The toughest issue Bush faced at the United Nations (UN) involved China. When the UN was formed in 1945, the Nationalist government of China was one of the five great powers (along with

Bush is sworn in as United States representative to the United Nations in 1971. President Richard Nixon is at the right.

the United States, the Soviet Union, Great Britain, and France). Then in 1949, after a bitter civil war, Chinese Communists took over and drove the Nationalists to Taiwan, an island off the Chinese coast. The new government introduced *Communism* (a system in which land and businesses are owned and controlled by the government), creating the People's Republic of China. Even though they no longer ruled China, the Nationalists kept their seat in the UN for more than 20 years.

By the time Bush became the U.S. ambassador, most world nations wanted to admit the People's Republic of China to the UN and to drop Nationalist China. The United States agreed that the People's Republic should be admitted, but argued that the Nationalists in Taiwan should keep their membership as well. Bush worked hard to gain support for the "dual representation" plan. In the end, he failed to convince enough delegates. The UN voted to admit the People's Republic and expel the Nationalists. Even so, Bush received praise from many UN delegates for his efforts to achieve a compromise.

Bush raises his hand to veto a resolution in the United Nations Security Council. The earphones provide simultaneous translation of speeches not made in English.

Not everyone was impressed with Bush's performance, however. At the end of 1971, *New York* magazine put him on its list of the "ten most overrated men in New York City." George and Barbara reacted with good humor, throwing a party for themselves and the nine other "overrated men."

"Not an Easy Job"

President Nixon won re-election in 1972 in an enormous landslide, carrying every state but Massachusetts. Soon after the results were in, the president began to reorganize his administration. He summoned Bush from New York and asked him to take on a new assignment—as chairman of the Republican National Committee (RNC). Trading the glamorous United Nations job for the RNC was not terribly appealing. Bush would have to deal with tough disputes within the party and follow orders from Nixon's White House staff. Barbara told George he'd be better off doing "anything but that." George, ever loyal to the party, said, "You can't turn a president down."

The assignment turned out to be even more difficult than Bush expected. Within months, the Nixon administration was overwhelmed by the Watergate scandal, in which high-ranking Republicans had been charged with serious wrongdoing. Soon Bush's main role was defending the president against Watergate charges. Nixon personally promised Bush that he had done nothing wrong. Taking the president at his word, Bush traveled the country defending the embattled president. Bush admitted, "It was not an easy job."

Bush wrote that when he learned the president had been covering up the Watergate burglary from the beginning, "I was deeply offended and amazed. After this I lost faith in Nixon." On August 6, 1974, Bush spoke up at a meeting of

The Watergate Scandal

In the early morning hours of June 17, 1972, five burglars were arrested in the offices of the Democratic National Committee in the Watergate office complex in Washington, D.C. They had cameras to photograph documents and listening devices to install on committee telephones. The story didn't attract much attention at first, but in 1973 it grew into the biggest political scandal in U.S. history.

Investigators showed that the burglars had ties to Nixon's re-election committee, which would help Nixon win his landslide victory in November 1972. In January 1973, it was revealed that the burglars had received their orders from Nixon's former attorney general and his top White House aides. Still, the president claimed innocence.

Soon it was revealed that Nixon campaign associates had carried out many other "dirty tricks" aimed at damaging the reputations of Democratic candidates and others they saw as enemies. The difficult question was whether the president was involved—in planning the actions or in trying to cover them up.

In July 1973, a White House assistant revealed that President Nixon had a secret system for recording his conversations in the White House. Watergate investigators immediately made official requests for the recorded conversations. Nixon refused to give them up at first, but was finally ordered to do so by the Supreme Court. One of these tapes revealed that Nixon had been involved in covering up the Watergate crimes from the beginning. The U.S. House of Representatives was preparing *articles of impeachment* (accusations of serious wrongdoing) against Nixon. Rather than face an impeachment trial and likely removal from office, Nixon resigned on August 9, 1974.

☆ ☆ ☆

President Nixon defends himself during the Watergate scandal in 1974. In August, he decided to resign rather than face an impeachment trial in the U.S. Senate.

Nixon's *cabinet* (heads of federal departments who gather to advise the president). He surprised those at the meeting by urging the president to resign. The following day, he joined a chorus of other voices in the Republican party, sending a public letter to the president advising resignation. On August 8, Nixon announced in a televised address that he would resign the next day. On August 9, Barbara and George attended the emotional farewell at the White House as Nixon and his family said good-bye. Nixon's vice president, Gerald Ford, was sworn in as the 38th president.

Following a recent Constitutional amendment, Ford was required to nominate a vice president to replace himself. Bush hoped he would be Ford's choice, but Ford chose New York governor Nelson Rockefeller instead. The new president offered Bush a high-ranking diplomatic assignment. Bush asked to be sent as chief liaison officer to the People's Republic of China.

Around the World and Back ─────────────

President Nixon began improving relations with China when he visited in 1972, yet China was still a mystery to most Westerners. To Bush, China seemed an exciting challenge—just the sort of adventure on which he thrived.

George and Barbara Bush arrived in Beijing, the Chinese capital, eager to make a contribution to international understanding. They took Chinese lessons five times a week. Rather than using official limousines, they sometimes rode bicycles through the streets of the city just as Chinese commuters did. Bush also decided it was important to socialize with the Chinese and other diplomats as much as possible. He and Barbara attended many official and unofficial gatherings, a pleasant surprise to Chinese officials. The previous U.S. liaison had avoided most social affairs.

They also made an impression with their dog, named C. Fred. Dogs were an unusual sight in Beijing in at the time. In earlier years, the government had forbidden dogs in the city to end the spread of serious diseases. People were hesitant to come near Fred. One of the first phrases Barbara learned in Chinese was, "Don't worry, he's only a little dog and he doesn't bite."

Bush's job included promoting trade with China, and building more friendly relations between the two countries. He also hosted a constant stream of

George and Barbara Bush with their bicycles in Beijing in 1974, when George Bush was chief U.S. liaison officer in China. Behind the Bushes is a portrait of Chinese leader Mao Zedong.

visitors, including U.S. leaders, family, and friends. When Secretary of State Henry Kissinger visited, he and Bush paid a visit to Chairman Mao Zedong, the aging Chinese leader. They were among the first Westerners granted a meeting with Mao.

In early November 1975, Bush received a cable instructing him to return to Washington. President Ford had nominated him to become the director of the Central Intelligence Agency (CIA). Once again, Bush was asked to leave a post he loved to take a more difficult assignment. As Bush later wrote, the CIA was in serious trouble, "battered by hostile congressional investigations, exposés, and charges that ran from lawbreaking to simple incompetence." Morale was low. Also, the job was considered a political dead end. No former intelligence director had ever run for higher office.

Bush testifies before the Senate Armed Services Committee after being nominated as Director of Central Intelligence.

Still, the president had asked, and Bush could not say no. During the year he was director he used his business skills to improve the way the CIA operated. He helped boost morale and restore unity within the organization. In the end, he found the position invigorating. He wrote to an old friend, "This is the most interesting job I've ever had."

Return to Politics

Bush's position as intelligence chief kept him on the sidelines in the 1976 presidential election. President Ford ran for a full term and was challenged by Democrat Jimmy Carter. Carter won the election. With the change of administrations, Carter would appoint a new intelligence director. Once again, Bush was out of a job.

The Bushes returned to Texas after an absence of six years. They bought a house in Houston, and George worked for a number of businesses as a consultant and board member. The work paid well and allowed Bush to travel, but he missed politics. Soon he began to consider running for president in 1980. He began campaigning quietly in 1978 and officially announced his candidacy on May 1, 1979. He believed that the Carter presidency was dampening the American spirit and that he could help restore the nation's confidence and optimism.

Bush's leading competitor for the nomination was California governor Ronald Reagan, a leader of the party's conservative wing. The first test of strength came in the Iowa *caucuses* (local meetings in which a party chooses its candidates). Bush's hard work paid off in a victory over the Reagan forces. An excited Bush told reporters that he had "the Big Mo," big momentum, in the campaign.

After three years out of government, George Bush campaigns for the Republican presidential nomination in 1980.

Reporters thought the slangy phrase sounded silly, and Bush's opponents used it against him. In this sour atmosphere, Bush entered the New Hampshire primary.

Then at a gathering in Nashua, Bush thought he had a chance to debate with Ronald Reagan. When four lesser candidates arrived unexpectedly to join the debate, Bush let his disappointment show. Reagan welcomed the other candidates, but according to one reporter, Bush sat resentfully on stage, looking "like a small boy who had been dropped off at the wrong birthday party." Reagan won the debate and soon afterward, he won the state primary, with 50 percent of the vote to Bush's 23 percent. Bush had lost "the Big Mo."

Bush won several primaries, but the steam had gone out of his campaign. Some things he said, however, made a lasting impression. In a speech given in Pennsylvania, he lambasted Reagan's economic program, based on reducing tax rates without decreasing government spending. Bush called this approach "voodoo economics." The phrase would come to haunt Bush, not his opponent.

Reagan proved to be the more appealing candidate. Republicans liked his conservative platform and his warm, friendly manner. His confidence and optimism made him a growing favorite. On May 30, 1980, Bush conceded defeat. He vowed to support a unified Republican effort to defeat Carter. Party leaders appreciated Bush's loyalty to his party and his willingness to support his opponent after a tough campaign.

An Unexpected Call

Former president Gerald Ford was also a loyal Reagan supporter. When the Republican convention opened in Detroit on July 14, 1980, most people assumed that Reagan would choose Ford as his vice-presidential running mate. Ford actively campaigned for the job, describing a Reagan-Ford ticket as a "dream team." Ford went a step too far, however, when he seemed to suggest that he would share the presidency with Reagan.

Angry at the suggestion that he needed a co-president, Reagan quietly took Ford's name off his list. That brought George Bush's name to the top. Reagan knew that Bush would be a strong vice-presidential candidate. He could help carry the state of Texas, he appealed to Republicans in parts of the country where Reagan was not as popular, and he was more experienced than Reagan in foreign policy.

The Bush family and friends were gathered in a hotel room awaiting Reagan's announcement of his vice-presidential candidate when the phone rang. Ronald Reagan was calling to ask Bush to be his candidate for vice president. Reagan asked if Bush could support the conservative Reagan agenda. Bush immediately told Reagan he could support it "wholeheartedly." Bush's critics complained that Bush had given up his own convictions in order to get ahead politically.

During the campaign, Reagan persuaded a majority of voters that he could bring needed change to America. The country was discouraged by high inflation,

Ronald Reagan, who defeated Bush for the presidential nomination, nominated Bush to run for vice president. Here they laugh together during campaign meetings.

high unemployment, and a long hostage crisis in Iran, where U.S. government employees had been held for more than a year. President Carter seemed unable to solve these problems, while Reagan appeared strong and reassuring. On election day voters swept Reagan and Bush into office. The pair won 44 states and 489 electoral votes. George and Barbara Bush would be moving back to Washington.

4

Settling In

Number One Observatory Circle, the vice president's official house in Washington, D.C., is perched high on a hill about 2.5 miles (4 kilometers) northwest of the White House. When the Bushes moved in, it was the 28th move they had made in 36 years. They would live longer there than in any other house since they were married.

According to the Constitution, a vice president's main role is to preside over the Senate and take over if the president becomes incapacitated. Following the practice of other recent presidents, Reagan gave Bush a variety of other responsibilities. The vice president became the head of government task forces to address such problems as international drug smuggling, terrorism, and illegal immigration.

Bush enjoyed regular access to the president. Soon after the inauguration, Reagan and Bush began a tradition of having lunch together on Thursdays—just the two of them, with no particular agenda. Since they both loved Mexican food, the lunches usually consisted of tortilla chips and salsa, followed by cheese soup or chili. Bush tried to bring a new joke to the table each week, knowing Reagan's fondness for humor.

Bush sometimes disagreed with Reagan's policies, and he discussed his disagreements with the president in private. In public, he remained a loyal Reagan supporter. Once he blurted out, "I'm for Mr. Reagan, blindly!" When critics made fun of such unquestioning loyalty, Bush answered that in his family, loyalty was "not considered a character flaw."

"Only the President Lands on the South Lawn"

On March 30, 1981, Bush was introduced to the most sobering responsibility of a vice president. That afternoon President Reagan delivered a speech at the Hilton Hotel in Washington. Leaving the building with his team, Reagan waved to the television cameras and headed toward his car. Suddenly, there was a loud *POP*. Then another and another—six gunshots in all. Reagan's aides and Secret Service men dove to protect the president and to stop the shooter, even as wounded men fell to the ground. Reagan had been shot. So had a Secret Service officer, a policeman, and Reagan's press secretary, Jim Brady. The would-be assassin, 25-year-old John Hinckley Jr., was caught immediately.

Reagan was hurried to George Washington University Hospital, where doctors discovered that a bullet had entered under his left arm and lodged in lung tissue less than an inch from his heart. They began to replace the blood the president had lost, then prepared to operate to remove the bullet and repair the damage. The surgery was successful. When Nancy Reagan visited her husband, Reagan was ready with a joke, saying, "Honey, I forgot to duck."

Bush learned of the assassination attempt just as the vice-presidential aircraft, *Air Force 2*, was taking off from Fort Worth, Texas, bound for Austin, Texas. Bush decided to refuel in Austin and head immediately back to Washington. When he arrived, the Secret Service suggested that Bush fly directly to the White House by helicopter. Bush refused the suggestion, concerned that it would give the impression he was swooping in to take over. "Only the president lands on the South Lawn," he said.

Bush arrived without fanfare at the White House by car at seven that evening. In his first meeting with presidential aides, he said, "The more normal things are, the better. . . . We want to make the government function as normally as possible." The next morning, Bush headed emergency meetings with the

Ronald Wilson Reagan

Born in the small town of Tampico, Illinois, Ronald Reagan (1911–2004) became one of the most popular presidents in United States history. After working as a radio announcer, he moved to Hollywood in 1937, where he became a leading movie actor. Over the next 30 years he acted in films and as the host of a popular television drama series.

Reagan first became active in politics as president of the Screen Actors Guild, the union representing movie actors. Beginning in the early 1960s, he took an active role in Republican politics and was elected governor of California in 1966 and 1970. In 1976 he ran for Republican presidential nomination against President Gerald Ford, but lost. By 1980, however, his message and his well-organized campaign swept him into office. He was re-elected in 1984.

President Ronald Reagan.

After his retirement in 1989, Reagan remained a beloved and widely admired figure. After a long struggle with Alzheimer's disease, he died on June 5, 2004. Former president Bush spoke at the funeral, calling him a "strong and gentle" friend.

☆ ☆ ☆

president's cabinet and with congressional leaders. He was careful to sit in his regular seat, and not in the president's place.

Four More Years ———————————————

During his tenure as vice president, Bush visited all 50 states and 75 nations, logging more than 1 million miles (1.6 million km) of travel. His foreign trips often involved attending government functions as the official U.S. representative and visiting U.S. troops stationed overseas. After a suicide bomber blew up a Marine barracks in Beirut, Lebanon, on October 23, 1983, Bush visited the scene of the disaster. He recalled that visit as "one of my most difficult and emotional assignments."

During his first term in office, Reagan continued to promise "an era of national renewal." Even though the difficult economic times persisted, people wanted to believe his confident and reassuring words. Reagan and Bush won the Republican nominations for re-election in 1984 without opposition, then faced Democrats Walter Mondale and Geraldine Ferraro in the general elections.

Ferraro, a longtime congresswoman from New York, was the first woman ever nominated for vice president on a major party ticket. Bush met Ferraro in a single vice-presidential debate and was criticized by many viewers who claimed that he seemed not to take Ferraro seriously. Meanwhile Reagan was having different problems. In a debate with Mondale, the president became muddled and

In the 1984 campaign, Bush debates Democratic vice-presidential nominee Geraldine Ferraro, the first woman ever nominated to that high office by a major political party.

confused. These fluffs turned out to be minor problems, however. Reagan led in all the public opinion polls, and his critics complained that he was the "Teflon President"—like food in a Teflon skillet, criticisms of his performance or policies never seemed to "stick."

Reagan and Bush won a landslide victory—carrying every state except Minnesota—and receiving 525 electoral votes to Mondale's 13. Vice President Bush was sworn in for a second time, inside the Capitol Rotunda. Bush clearly loved his position, saying, "I can't wait to get to work every day. I've got plenty to do, and I feel comfortable in my job."

In July 1985, Bush was faced once again with the possibility that he might be called upon to serve as president. President Reagan underwent surgery to remove cancerous growths in his large intestine. For the first time, a U.S. administration followed provisions of the 25th Amendment that provide for an acting president when the president is unable to carry out his duties. For eight hours on July 13, 1985, President Reagan was unconscious during and after his surgery. During that time, George Bush served as the first acting president.

Iran-Contra Affair ───────────────

Much of Reagan's second term in office was clouded by a series of shady dealings known as the Iran-Contra affair. It involved two secret White House operations that began in 1985. The first involved providing U.S. government support for the "Contras," who were carrying on a civil war against the socialist government of Nicaragua. Congress had passed a law prohibiting U.S. government support of the Contras, but high officials in the Reagan administration arranged to provide support secretly. Then in October 1986, the Nicaraguan government shot down a plane filled with weapons and captured an American crewman, who confessed that the plane had been delivering the weapons to the Contras.

The second operation involved selling weapons to Iran, even though the U.S. government had placed an *embargo* (a prohibition) on selling arms to that country. At first, the weapon sales were payments to Iran to release U.S. hostages they had taken. In November 1986, a Middle Eastern newspaper reported that Iran had released an American hostage in return for a shipment of arms. Investigations in the United States proved that the story was true. Later, selling arms to Iran and delivering support to Contras in Nicaragua were linked. The money Iran paid for some weapons was secretly used to buy military supplies for the Contras in Nicaragua.

When these secret operations came to light, Americans wanted to know who authorized the arms-for-hostages dealings. Did the president know? What about the vice president? At first Reagan denied the accusations, but he later admitted knowing about and giving his approval of the sale of arms to Iran. Vice

President Bush was present when Reagan approved this deal. Reagan or Bush may also have known that money from the sale of weapons to Iran was being used to fund the Contras. Bush denied knowing anything about dealings with the Contras, claiming he had been "out of the loop" when decisions were made.

Several Reagan officials confessed to or were convicted of crimes in the Iran-Contra matter and sent to prison. Democrats proposed an impeachment inquiry into Reagan's role. In March 1987, the president publicly accepted responsibility for his actions and those of his administration. The public seemed to lose interest in further investigations, and Reagan proved again to be the Teflon President. Bush managed to stay just out of the spotlight.

"Read My Lips"

By late 1987, George Bush's attention had shifted to running for the presidency in 1988. On October 13, 1987, Bush announced his candidacy in Houston. He explained that his campaign would not head in "radical new directions" but would continue to provide "strong and steady leadership."

That same week, Bush appeared on the cover of *Newsweek* magazine. Near his photo on the cover was the headline "FIGHTING THE WIMP FACTOR." The story inside was not flattering. It discussed Bush's image as a rich, preppy, nice guy without a clear idea of what he wanted to accomplish. Bush had faced this kind of criticism since his early campaigns in Texas. On the eve of his presidential campaign, however, the criticisms stung more than ever. "The *Newsweek* story was the cheapest shot I've seen in my political life," he wrote in his diary.

As his campaign manager, Bush engaged Lee Atwater, one of the toughest campaign planners in the business. Atwater set out to toughen Bush's image, and wipe out the "Wimp Factor." Instead of being courteous to everyone, Bush sometimes snapped at interviewers. He appeared in New Hampshire driving an 18-wheeler truck and wearing a wool shirt. In addition, his advertisements against other Republican candidates were sharp and negative. Bush won the New Hampshire primary, and on "Super Tuesday," when primaries were held in 16 states, he swept them all, assuring his nomination at the Republican convention. Even so, Bush still had critics in his own party. Conservatives remembered that he had called Reagan's policy of lowering taxes "voodoo economics." Moderates recalled how quickly he changed his tune when he had the chance to run as Reagan's vice president. Bush still had much to prove.

At the Republican convention, Bush gave the best-remembered speech of his career. In it he promised to continue the peace and prosperity of the Reagan years. He called for more volunteers to serve in their communities, reciting a long list of voluntary civic and religious organizations in local communities. These volunteers, he said, are "like stars, like a thousand points of light in a broad and peaceful sky." At another point, he said, "I want a kinder and gentler nation."

Bush combined his rosy view of America with a famous promise not to raise taxes. "The Congress will push me to raise taxes and I'll say 'no.' And they'll push, and I'll say 'no.' And they'll push again, and I'll say to them, 'Read my lips: no new taxes!'"

The Democrats nominated Governor Michael Dukakis of Massachusetts for president. Dukakis had improved his state's economy during the Reagan recession years, a feat dubbed the "Massachusetts Miracle." He pledged to do the same for the rest of the country. As his running mate, Dukakis chose Texas senator Lloyd Bentsen, the conservative Democrat who had beaten Bush out of a Senate seat in 1970.

Bush's running mate, Senator Dan Quayle of Indiana, brought to the ticket a brand of conservatism that Bush hoped would win the votes of far-right Republicans. Quayle lacked national campaign experience, however, and was easily rattled. He soon became the butt of Democratic jokes.

Bush may have wanted a kinder and gentler America, but he and Lee Atwater did not want a kinder and gentler campaign. The Bush team attacked Dukakis's character and patriotism, and accused him of being soft on crime. Their ads spotlighted a prison furlough program in Massachusetts, which allowed

In 1988 presidential candidate George Bush waves to the Republican convention with his vice-presidential running mate, Dan Quayle of Indiana.

selected prisoners to have unsupervised weekends away from prison. One of these felons had escaped and committed another violent crime. The Bush campaign produced a television advertisement showing a silent line of prisoners going through a revolving turnstile, walking into a prison and right back out. A voice-over said, "Michael Dukakis says he wants to do for America what he's done for Massachusetts. America can't afford that risk."

Dukakis had not been expecting such venom from the Bush team and was put on the defensive. He and his campaign managers attacked Bush in return. They accused him of having no particular vision for the country. Perhaps this lack of larger issues caused lack of interest in the election. On election day, the smallest percentage of eligible voters came to the polls since 1924: just under 50 percent. Of those who voted, more than 53 percent chose George Bush. Bush won 40 states with 426 electoral votes to Dukakis's 10 states and the District of Columbia with a total of 112 electoral votes. Bush became the first sitting vice president to be elected president since Martin Van Buren in 1836.

For George Bush, the most exciting phase of his life was just beginning. It was time to move yet again, this time into the White House.

Chapter 5

First Days

Inauguration day in January 1989 dawned cold but clear. As George H. W. Bush repeated the oath of office, he marveled at the historical distinction of the event. Just 200 years earlier, in 1789, George Washington was sworn in as the nation's first president. Barbara Bush held two Bibles for her husband to use in the ceremony. One was the Bush family Bible; the other was the Bible used by George Washington at his inaugural. Bush's mother, Dorothy Walker Bush, was also on the inaugural stand. Now 87 years old, she watched proudly as her son pledged to work for peace. His goal as president, he said, was to "make kinder the face of the nation and gentler the face of the world."

The morning after the inauguration, George and Barbara held an open house at the White House, the first since 1909. Thousands

George and Barbara Bush in the Oval Office. Their dog Millie is at bottom right.

wanted a chance to tour the mansion. When the president looked out his window that morning he saw "people all over the darn place. They'd spent the night there." The first 15 in line got an extra bonus: a private tour conducted by the new first family.

Bush quickly settled into a "workaholic" routine, rising at 5:30 each morning to read the newspapers and arriving in his office at 7:00. His staff described him as having unyielding energy. Secretary of State James Baker said he had "the finest manners of any man you'll ever meet, but somewhere along the way he never learned to sit still."

Meanwhile, George and Barbara Bush brought a low-key style to the White House, filling it with frequent visits from their many grandchildren. Bush had a horseshoe pit installed on the lawn, and many days could be found pitching "shoes" with White House staff. Reporters appreciated that Bush would speak off the cuff to them, sometimes while taking his daily jog. One day he mentioned that he hated broccoli. Now that he was president, he said, he didn't have to eat it anymore. The comment pleased and amused millions of Americans, but the broccoli farmers didn't think it was so funny. They expressed their protest by sending the president a truckload of broccoli. The Bushes donated the vegetable to Washington food banks.

During her first year as first lady, Barbara Bush was sometimes criticized about her "matronly" appearance. She had a smart answer for her critics: "My mail tells me a lot of fat, white-haired wrinkled ladies are tickled pink." Barbara's quick wit was a welcome addition to the White House. An extremely popular first lady, she was admired for her unaffected appearance, her informal approach to entertaining, and her unflagging commitment to good causes.

Barbara Bush's favorite cause was family literacy. "I strongly believe that if every man, woman, and child in America could read, write, and comprehend," she said, "we would be much closer to solving many of our nation's serious problems." While in the White House, she wrote a best-selling children's book and donated the proceeds to her foundation for family literacy.

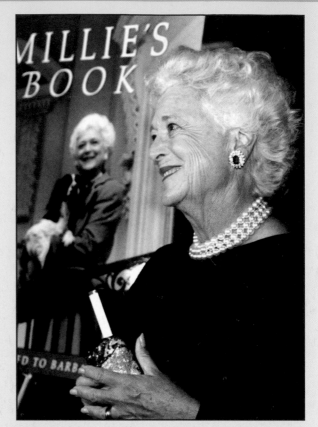

Barbara Bush promotes *Millie's Book,* the best seller supposedly by the Bush dog "as dictated to Barbara Bush."

Throughout her husband's political career, Barbara stood steadfastly by his side, helping on each step of the way. While some criticized her for never following a career separate from her husband's, Barbara always said that she was happy with her choices and did not regret her decisions. Barbara and George Bush agreed that family is the most important thing in life. She adored spending time with their children and later with their 14 grandchildren.

Early Bumps

Bush's early days in office did not go smoothly. One of his first nominations for a cabinet position was Texas senator John Tower as secretary of defense. Tower was a personal friend and a staunch Republican. It turned out in Senate hearings, however, that Tower was not popular with many of his colleagues and that he had a reputation as a heavy drinker and a womanizer. To Bush's embarrassment, the Senate rejected the nomination. His second choice for defense, Congressman Richard Cheney, was quickly approved. Cheney had already served as chief of staff to President Ford and would later be elected vice president on a ticket with George Bush's son in 2000 and 2004.

A second crisis had been brewing for years. During Reagan's presidency, savings and loan associations, banks that specialized in lending money to consumers to buy homes, received government permission to invest their funds in other ventures. Hundreds of these banks invested unwisely and began to falter. If they were allowed to fail, millions of ordinary Americans would be hurt. Bush worked with Congress to help the damaged industry. In August 1989, Congress passed the Financial Institutions Reform, Recovery, and Enforcement Act, approving a bailout plan that would cost the government $50 billion. The cost increased the already large federal deficit.

International Crises

Bush was soon required to deal with major developments overseas. On June 4, 1989, hundreds of Chinese student protesters were gathered in Tiananmen Square, in the center of Beijing, China, to demand democratic reforms in the Chinese government. The world watched in horror as Chinese troops cleared the square with tanks, killing dozens of protesters. The Bush administration was put in a delicate situation. Bush was sickened by the tragedy, but he was also determined not to let this incident destroy the country's relationship with China. He quietly condemned China's actions and imposed mild penalties on the Chinese government. Critics were disappointed that he did not speak more forcefully and that he did not impose more significant penalties.

Since his days as CIA director, Bush had been a strong supporter of actions to end the smuggling of cocaine and other drugs into the United States. He singled out Manuel Noriega, then the dictatorial president of Panama, as one of the chief managers of the drug traffic, calling him "the number one public enemy." In October 1989, Noriega was nearly overthrown by Panamanians supported by the U.S. government, but he managed to survive and punish his enemies. On December 16, an American soldier in Panama was killed after being stopped at a military checkpoint in Panama, and a U.S. navy lieutenant and his wife were kidnapped and beaten. These incidents persuaded Bush to act.

Chinese tanks begin rolling across Tiananmen Square in Beijing in June 1989. Thousands of students were camping on the square in tents, protesting government policies.

Fall of the Berlin Wall

Since 1949, Germany was divided into West Germany, an ally of the United States, and East Germany, which was closely supervised by the Soviet Union. Soon after the division, East Germans began migrating to West Germany, seeking greater opportunity and freedom. Many walked across the border from East Berlin to West Berlin, which was an "island" of West Germany surrounded by East German territory. Finally, to end this outflow of people, East German authorities built a wall dividing East and West Berlin in 1961.

The wall was a massive barrier made of stone and concrete and topped with barbed wire. It was patrolled by armed guards, who had killed nearly 200 people trying to escape to the West. In June 1987, President Reagan had spoken in West Berlin, urging Soviet leader Mikhail Gorbachev to "tear down this wall." Now, in 1989, the Soviet Union was losing control over its *satellite states* (small countries dominated by a large powerful nation nearby), including East Germany.

On the evening of November 9, 1989, the East German government announced that travel restrictions between East and West had been lifted. Thousands of celebrating Germans gathered on both sides side of the wall. They walked freely through the checkpoints and began to attack the wall itself with hammers and chisels.

The fall of the Berlin Wall came to symbolize the collapse of the Soviet empire. The following year, East and West Germany joined to form a reunited Germany, and in 1999, Berlin became the unified nation's capital.

☆☆☆

Germans gather to help tear down the Berlin Wall on November 10, 1989, after travel restrictions between East and West Germany were canceled.

Just after midnight on December 20, 14,000 U.S. troops landed in Panama to capture Noriega. By the next morning, the fighting was over. Hundreds of Panamanians and 25 Americans were killed. Noriega disappeared, but was found a few days later in the Vatican Embassy in Panama City. He surrendered to U.S. troops on January 3, 1990, and was brought to Miami to stand trial. Convicted on eight counts of drug trafficking and money laundering, he was sentenced to a 40-year prison term. Bush's decisive action boosted his popularity in the United States, but critics complained that the operation cost too many lives.

The Budget Compromise

When Bush took office, the federal *deficit* was $170 billion (the government spent $170 billion more than it took in that year). The deficit had ballooned during the Reagan administration. Bush's first year in office saw inflation rising. The stock market, which had been rising nicely through the year, plunged on October 13, frightening investors even though stock prices recovered quickly. As 1990 began, there were more signs of a recession. More workers were unemployed, and business activity was down. Something had to be done.

That something was a tax increase. Finally, after meetings with congressional leaders, Bush agreed on June 26, 1990, to a bill that would increase taxes.

Forced to break his campaign promise of no new taxes, Bush faced loud criticism. The *New York Post* headline read, "READ MY LIPS: I LIED." Many Americans were angry that Bush had broken his promise and raised their taxes. Others were angry that the increase was much too small to bring down the deficit. The deficit continued to climb, reaching $290 billion by 1992.

Operation Desert Storm

On August 1, 1990, Bush was getting a deep-heat treatment for sore shoulders. His moment of relaxation was interrupted by an aide, who reported that troops of Iraq were massed on the border of their neighbor Kuwait, poised to invade. An hour later, some 140,000 Iraqi troops and 18,000 tanks crossed the border, and within 12 hours, Iraqi leader Saddam Hussein proclaimed Kuwait a part of Iraq.

"What Iraq has done violates every norm of international law," Bush declared. Within hours he began calling world leaders, seeking support for actions to force Iraq to retreat and to restore Kuwait's independence. He received expressions of support from many nations, including the Soviet Union.

"This will not stand, this aggression against Kuwait," the president told reporters on August 5. Three days later he made it official in a televised speech. He declared that Americans wanted nothing less than "the immediate, unconditional, and complete withdrawal of all Iraqi forces from Kuwait." Later that day he told a news conference, "A line has been drawn in the sand."

U.S. ally Saudi Arabia, which bordered both Iraq and Kuwait, agreed to let allied forces use its territory as a staging ground. Bush hoped that by sending a strong force to Saudi Arabia, the world could persuade Iraq to withdraw from Kuwait. As the coalition began assembling troops, however, Saddam added to his troops in Kuwait and southern Iraq. On November 29, 1990, the United Nations Security Council ordered Iraq to withdraw from Kuwait by January 15, 1991. The world waited in suspense to see if the Iraqis would withdraw. If they refused, a huge force of coalition troops was prepared to drive them out by military force.

When the deadline passed, the Iraqi army had not budged. U.S. General Norman Schwarzkopf, the commander of the coalition forces, launched a massive air attack on the morning of January 17. Operation Desert Storm had begun. Television viewers around the world followed the campaign through live reports from the front and from Baghdad, behind enemy lines. New laser-guided bombing technology gave the U.S. Air Force the ability to lock in on their targets with the precision of a video game, and some called the bombardment the "Nintendo War." The shelling continued for nearly six weeks. The Iraqis retaliated by

President Bush and U.S. General Norman Schwarzkopf review the military build-up in Saudi Arabia before the beginning of the Persian Gulf War in November 1990.

releasing millions of gallons of Kuwait's oil into the Persian Gulf and setting fire

to its oil wells.

On February 24, American ground troops entered Kuwait. In just 100 hours

(about four days and nights), the fighting was over. The Iraqi army had been driven

Fast Facts

THE PERSIAN GULF WAR

Who: Iraq against a U.S.-led coalition of about 50 countries

When: January 16, 1991, to February 27, 1991

Where: Kuwait, Iraq

Why: To drive Iraqi troops from Kuwait, which Iraq had occupied by force

Outcome: Coalition forces carried out a 39-day bombing attack on Iraqi military targets, then began a massive ground attack on February 24. Within a little more than four days and nights, Iraqis were driven out of Kuwait and surrendered. U.S. casualties numbered 146 killed and 467 wounded; the rest of the coalition lost 98 soldiers. Iraqi casualties (dead, wounded, and missing) were estimated at 10,000.

Interesting Fact: The air pollution from oil fires or exposure to radioactive wastes may have caused "Gulf War syndrome," mysterious ailments that afflicted many veterans of the war in the years to come.

from Kuwait into the deserts of southern Iraq. On February 27, President Bush spoke to the nation from the Oval Office. "Kuwait is liberated. Iraq's army is defeated," he said. "It is a time of pride, pride in our troops, pride in the friends who stood with us in the crisis, pride in our nation."

Bush's popularity soared. According to *USA Today*, his approval rating reached 91 percent, the highest ever recorded for president. Patriotism blossomed across the country, and the troops returned home to enthusiastic and welcoming crowds. There were critics though, who said that the coalition stopped too soon. Saddam Hussein remained in power. In coming months he would turn on ethnic minorities in Iraq, killing additional thousands. Even so, Bush defended his actions and pointed out that the coalition had accomplished its mission.

U.S. Marines with gas masks on patrol near giant oil fires in Kuwait during the Persian Gulf War in February 1991.

Historic Times

The fall of the Berlin Wall in 1989 was only the beginning of the changes taking place in Europe and the Soviet Union. After more than 40 years, the *Cold War* (a military, political, and economic competition between the United States and the Soviet Union) was coming to an end as the Soviet Union's power rapidly diminished. Former Soviet satellites Poland, Hungary, and Czechoslovakia all opened their borders, and began to introduce government reforms. The Soviet Union still had a large army, but it was in no position to crush uprisings outside its borders. The republics that made up the Soviet Union itself were beginning to move toward independence. In addition, the Soviet economy was grinding to a halt. Soviet leader Mikhail Gorbachev promoted economic reforms to help revive the economy, but they only weakened the government's hold on its outlying territories.

In December 1989, Bush and Gorbachev met near the Mediterranean island of Malta. An unusually strong storm with gale-force winds kept the leaders apart on the first night, but when they did meet, they established a friendly relationship and improved relations between their countries. By 1991, the Soviet Union was dissolving, as its many republics declared independence from the government in Moscow. The U.S. government established diplomatic relations with

Soviet President Mikhail Gorbachev and President Bush laugh together during a meeting in Helsinki, Finland.

each of the new independent countries. On December 25, 1991, Mikhail Gorbachev, now leader only of Russia, the largest Soviet republic, resigned from office. This marked the end of the Soviet Union. Bush wrote, "Our onetime greatest enemy no longer existed. The Cold War was officially over."

On the Home Front ———————————————————

Although foreign policy was President Bush's strength, several domestic achievements stand out. In 1990, he signed the Clean Air Act, which set stricter standards for how much pollution could be released by cars and factories. The same year, he signed the Americans with Disabilities Act, prohibiting discrimination against people with disabilities in the workplace and in housing.

Yet all was not smooth sailing. In 1991 Bush nominated Clarence Thomas to a seat on the Supreme Court. Thomas was an African American with strong conservative views. During his confirmation hearings Thomas faced bitter opposition from Democratic senators. In televised hearings, he was accused of sexual harassment by a former employee, law professor Anita Hill. Republican defenders responded by attacking Anita Hill's reputation, infuriating many women. Bush stood by his nominee, and Thomas was confirmed by a Senate vote of 52 to 48. However, the circuslike hearings and Thomas's controversial views hurt Bush in his campaign for re-election.

The economy, which had slipped into recession through mid-1991, was improving, but unemployment remained high. Especially in cities, crime, drug abuse, and homelessness were on the rise. By the summer of 1992, only 29 percent of people in public opinion polls approved of Bush's performance as president. The fight for the 1992 election was going to be tough.

Chapter **6**

Campaign Pains

Looking back, George Bush called 1992 the "worst year of my life." His problems began early in the year, when he announced his run for re-election. He was soon attacked by conservative Republican challenger Patrick Buchanan, a former adviser to presidents Nixon, Ford, and Reagan. Buchanan claimed that Bush seemed not to understand that the economy was hurting so many Americans.

Bush's old campaign manager Lee Atwater had died in 1991. As a result, Bush's campaign was slow to get started. In the first major Republican primary in New Hampshire, Bush won, but Buchanan, who had never held an elective office, captured 37 percent of the vote. The Bush campaign improved, and Buchanan's support faded in later primaries. At the Republican convention in the summer of 1992, Bush won the nomination easily.

In the days after the war against Iraq, many leading Democrats decided that Bush would be too strong to beat in 1992 and chose not to seek the Democratic nomination. One who continued to campaign was Arkansas governor Bill Clinton. Clinton seemed to have little chance early in the primary season, but made a surprisingly strong showing in New Hampshire. Calling himself the "the Comeback Kid," he went on to win the Democratic nomination. Clinton was young, good-looking, bright, and full of energy. In addition he had a kind of personal magnetism that thrilled crowds.

Clinton crisscrossed the nation, criticizing the Bush administration for its role in the sagging economy. He told unemployed workers and those working two jobs to make ends meet that he could "feel their pain," promising to end the recession and create more jobs. Bush, who had hoped to concentrate on his achievements in foreign policy, soon realized that voters were now more concerned with bread-and-butter issues at home. The Bush campaign decided to respond to the Clinton challenge by questioning Clinton's character. The campaign publicized accusations that Clinton had had affairs with women outside his marriage and that he had dishonestly avoided the draft during the Vietnam War. Bush asked the country, "Who do you trust?"

The 1992 campaign was complicated and enlivened by a strong third-party candidate. On February 20, billionaire Texas businessman Ross Perot entered the

George Bush debates with Democratic candidate Bill Clinton during the 1992 presidential campaign. Clinton defeated Bush's run for re-election.

race as the candidate of his own Independent party. Perot complained bitterly about the failure of the government in Washington to reduce huge government deficits. He promised voters that he would clean house and make the government more productive and more responsive to the people. Soon he was running nearly even with Bush and Clinton in opinion polls. Perot might have had a slight chance to win the election, but in July, he seemed to get cold feet. He withdrew from the race to protect his family's privacy, disappointing many of his supporters.

On October 1, Perot entered the race again, just in time to participate in three presidential debates. In the first debate he gained back much of his following, seeming more entertaining and persuasive than Bush or Clinton. In later debates, Clinton showed his debating skills and his broad knowledge of the issues. Only Bush seemed ill at ease. At one point, cameras caught him glancing at his watch while Clinton was talking, seeming to count the seconds until the debate was over.

On the afternoon of election day, the president received bad news from George W., his oldest son, who was managing the campaign. Early polls of people leaving their voting places showed that Clinton would defeat Bush by about five percentage points. When the votes were counted, Clinton received 43 percent of the vote to Bush's 38 percent and Perot's 19 percent. Clinton won 38 states and 370 electoral votes to Bush's 12 states and 168 electoral votes.

The 41st president, George H. W. Bush.

Bush was deeply disappointed by his poor showing. "It hurts," he said to adviser Colin Powell. "It really hurts to be rejected."

Not all in the Bush family were so unhappy. The day after the election, two of Bush's young granddaughters raced up to him and covered him with hugs. They said they were glad he lost because now they could spend more time with him.

In his last several weeks as president, Bush brought an end to the long controversy over the Iran-Contra matter. He pardoned several participants in the scandal, including former secretary of defense Caspar Weinberger, who had not yet been tried. On a more positive note, Bush sent American forces to the African nation of Somalia, where thousands of Somalis were on the brink of starvation during a brutal civil war. The troops distributed food and supplies on "a mission of peace and hope." It was a fitting way to end the presidency for a man who wanted to put a kinder face on the nation.

A Busy Retirement

On January 20, 1993, after attending Bill Clinton's inauguration, George and Barbara Bush were once again private citizens. They moved back to Houston to settle in a house they had recently built.

"We plan to get into the grandchildren business now," Bush said. With 14 grandchildren, they devoted a lot of time to this "business," both in Texas and at

First Dog

Leaving the White House with the Bushes was their dog Millie, one of the most popular White House pets in history. A brown-and-white springer spaniel, Millie was petted by world leaders, played with by famous politicians, and allowed the run of the White House. She sometimes slept in George and Barbara's bed. In 1990 she gained even more notoriety when the book she "dictated" to Barbara Bush, *Millie's Book*, became a best seller.

☆☆☆

Kennebunkport, Maine, where they still spent their summers. Bush wrote two books after leaving office: a collection of letters and a book on the end of the Cold War, co-written with former aide Brent Scowcroft. His office in Houston received hundreds of invitations to speak at a wide variety of events around the world.

In 1997 the George Bush Presidential Library opened in College Station, Texas, on the campus of Texas A&M University. In the spring of 1999, the Central Intelligence Agency honored Bush by naming its headquarters the George Bush Center for Intelligence.

Bush found life after the presidency comfortable and full. He continued his active lifestyle into old age, enjoying tennis and fishing. On his 75th birthday in 1999 he skydived from a plane solo. On his 80th birthday in 2004, he skydived again over the presidential library in College Station. This time he was tethered to a partner. After landing safely, Bush was enthusiastic. "For me, I like speed," he said. "I like the thrill of it. Just because you're 80 years old, it doesn't mean you're out of it."

A Second Bush Presidency

George Bush had decided to run for office in 1964, soon after his father retired from the U.S. Senate. In 1994, soon after he retired from the presidency, two of his own sons ran for governor in large, influential states, Jeb Bush in Florida, and George W. Bush in Texas. Jeb lost his race, but George W. Bush defeated popular Texas governor Ann Richards. In 1998, Jeb was elected governor in Florida, and George W. was re-elected in Texas.

In 2000, George W. Bush won the Republican nomination for president. In a close and controversial election, he defeated Democrat Al Gore. George and Barbara Bush were there to applaud their son when he was inaugurated in 2001. Bush was elected to a second term in 2004.

George and George W. Bush were only the second father-son presidential combination in the country's history. The first pair were John Adams (the second president, served 1797–1801) and his son John Quincy Adams (the sixth president, served 1825–1829).

On election night in 2000, Bush follows returns with presidential candidate George W. Bush and Florida governor Jeb Bush. George W. won the election, but the result was not known for sure for many weeks.

Legacy

The first George Bush was president during an eventful time in world affairs. The countries of Eastern Europe, long dominated by the Soviet Union, declared their independence from the Soviets and set up new political and economic systems. Soon afterward, the Soviet Union itself collapsed, resulting in a realignment of world diplomacy and more than a dozen new nations. Bush worked closely with the last Soviet leader, Mikhail Gorbachev, and supported leaders of new nations, but did not take an active role in these changes.

Bush did take an active role in the Middle East. After Iraqi armies attacked Kuwait, he helped gather the coalition that forced the Iraqis to withdraw. With the support of the United Nations and a broad coalition, the U.S. military carried out a brief and successful war. Beyond this single crusade, Bush was a "guardian president," reacting cautiously and avoiding any disasters at home and overseas.

On one of his last days as president, Bush wrote, "I hope history will show I did some things right." He will be remembered not as a brilliant leader, but as a president who was strongly patriotic, deeply respectful of the office he held, and loyal to his party. He guided the nation successfully through major world changes. History will conclude that he did many things right.

Fast Facts

George Herbert Walker Bush

Birth:	June 12, 1924
Birthplace:	Milton, Massachusetts
Parents:	Prescott Sheldon Bush and Dorothy Walker Bush
Sisters & Brothers:	Prescott Sheldon Jr. (1922–)
	Nancy (1926–)
	Jonathan James (1931–)
	William H. T. (Bucky) (1938–)
Education:	Phillips Academy, Andover, Massachusetts, graduated 1942
	Yale University, graduated 1948
Occupation:	Businessman, politician
Marriage:	To Barbara Pierce, January 6, 1945
Children:	(*see* First Lady Fast Facts at right)
Political Party:	Republican
Government Service:	1967–1971 Member, U.S. House of Representatives
	1971–1973 U.S. Ambassador to the United Nations
	1974–1975 U.S. Liaison to People's Republic of China
	1975–1976 Director of Central Intelligence Agency
	1981–1989 Vice President of the United States
	1989–1993 President of the United States
His Vice President:	J. Danforth Quayle
Major Actions as President:	1989 Ordered the invasion of Panama to overthrow and capture dictator Manuel Noriega
	1990 Signed the Americans with Disabilities Act
	1990 Signed the Clean Air Act
	1990 Assembled a coalition of nations against Iraq
	1991 Liberated Kuwait in the Persian Gulf War
	1992 Sent U.S. troops to Somalia as a peacekeeping force
Firsts:	First person to serve as acting president (July 13, 1985, when President Reagan was in surgery)

Fast Facts

Barbara Pierce Bush

Birth:	June 8, 1925
Birthplace:	New York, New York
Parents:	Marvin Pierce and Pauline Robinson Pierce
Sisters & Brothers:	Martha Ann (1920–1999)
	James (1922–1993)
	Scott (1930–)
Education:	Ashley Hall, Charleston, South Carolina, graduated 1943
	Smith College, Northampton, Massachusetts, attended 1943–1944
Marriage:	To George Herbert Walker Bush, January 6, 1945
Children:	George Walker Bush (1946–)
	Pauline Robinson (Robin) Bush (1949–1953)
	John Ellis (Jeb) Bush (1953–)
	Neil Mallon Bush (1955–)
	Marvin Pierce Bush (1956–)
	Dorothy Walker (Doro) Bush (1959–)

Timeline

1924	1925	1942	1943	1944

1924 — George Herbert Walker Bush born in Milton, Massachusetts, to Prescott and Dorothy Walker Bush, June 12.

1925 — Bush family moves to Greenwich, Connecticut.

1942 — Bush graduates from Phillips Andover Academy, enlists in U.S. Navy.

1943 — Enters World War II combat as navy aviator.

1944 — Bush plane is shot down in Pacific; he is rescued by submarine.

1954	1962	1964	1966	1970

1954 — Becomes proprietor of Zapata Off-Shore Company.

1962 — Elected chairman of the Republican party of Harris County, Texas.

1964 — Defeated in U.S. Senate race by Democrat Ralph Yarborough.

1966 — Sells interest in Zapata; elected to the House of Representatives; re-elected 1968.

1970 — Defeated in Senate race by Democrat Lloyd Bentsen.

1980	1988	1989	1990	1991

1980 — Elected vice president under Ronald Reagan; re-elected 1984.

1988 — Elected 41st president of the United States.

1989 — Meets with Mikhail Gorbachev at Malta summit; sends U.S. troops to Panama to capture General Manuel Noriega.

1990 — Signs Clean Air Act and Americans with Disabilities Act; mobilizes coalition to end Iraq's occupation of Kuwait.

1991 — Launches Persian Gulf War to liberate Kuwait; defeats Iraqi forces in 100-hour ground war.

1945	1946	1948	1951	1953

1945
Marries Barbara Pierce, January 6; discharged from navy; enters Yale.

1946
Oldest son, George Walker Bush, is born.

1948
Bush graduates from Yale; begins work in Texas oil business.

1951
Becomes a founder of Bush-Overbey Oil Development Company.

1953
Becomes a founder of Zapata Petroleum Corporation.

1971	1973	1974	1975	1976

1971
Appointed U.S. ambassador to the United Nations by President Nixon.

1973
Appointed chairman of the Republican National Committee.

1974
Appointed head of the U.S. Liaison Office in China by President Ford.

1975
Appointed director of the Central Intelligence Agency by President Ford.

1976
Resigns as CIA director after Democrat Jimmy Carter is elected president.

1992	1997

1992
Defeated in presidential election by Bill Clinton.

1997
Opens the George Bush Presidential Library in College Station, Texas.

Glossary

articles of impeachment: official charges of wrongdoing against a president or other official by Congress; if convicted of impeachment charges, the official is removed from office

cabinet: heads of federal government departments who meet to advise the president

caucus: a local or regional meeting of a political party, especially a meeting to choose the party's nominees for a future election

Cold War: military, political, and economic competition between the United States and the Soviet Union lasting from 1945 to 1991; both sides had powerful nuclear weapons but never engaged in an all-out (or "hot") war

Communism: a political and economic system in which land and businesses are owned and controlled by the government

deficit: the difference between how much a government or business spends in a year and how much it brings in; a shortfall

embargo: a government prohibition on selling goods or trading with another nation

satellite state: a small country whose government is dominated by a large powerful nation nearby

Further Reading

Bush, Barbara. *Millie's Book: As Dictated to Barbara Bush*. New York: William Morrow, 1990.

Green, Robert. *George Bush: Business Executive and U.S. President*. Chicago: Ferguson Publishing, 2000.

Greenberg, Judith E. *Barbara Pierce Bush, 1925–* . New York: Children's Press, 1999.

O'Shei, Tim, and Joe Marren. *George H. W. Bush*. Berkeley Heights, NJ: Enslow, 2002.

Schuman, Michael. *George H. W. Bush*. Berkeley Heights, NJ: MyReportLinks.com Books, 2003.

MORE ADVANCED READING

Bush, Barbara. *Barbara Bush: A Memoir*. New York: Charles Scribner's Sons, 1994.

Bush, George. *All the Best, George Bush: My Life in Letters and Other Writings*. New York: Scribner, 1999.

Greene, John Robert. *The Presidency of George Bush*. Lawrence: University Press of Kansas, 2000.

Parmet, Herbert S. *George Bush: The Life of a Lone Star Yankee*. New York: Scribner, 1997.

Wicker, Tom. *George Herbert Walker Bush*. New York: Lipper/Viking, 2004.

Places to Visit

★ ★ ★ ★ ★

The Capitol Building
Constitution Avenue
Washington, DC 20510
Visitor information: (202) 225-6827

George Bush served here in the House of Representatives from 1967 to 1971.

**George Bush Presidential Library
  and Museum**
1000 George Bush Drive West
College Station, TX 77845
(979) 691-4000
http://bushlibrary.tamu.edu/

Visit this state-of-the-art museum and see such items as a World War II Avenger torpedo bomber, George Bush's speedboat, artifacts from the 41st presidency, and changing exhibits on the former president and first lady.

The White House
1600 Pennsylvania Avenue NW
Washington, DC 20500
Visitors' Office: (202) 456-7041
http://www.whitehouse.gov

Tour the White House, George Bush's home from 1989 to 1993.

Online Sites of Interest

★ **The American Presidency**

http://gi.grolier.com/presidents

This site provides biographical information on the presidents at different reading levels, based on material in Scholastic/Grolier encyclopedias.

★ **The American President**

http://www.americanpresident.org/history/georgehwbush/

Provides valuable information on the life and times of U.S. presidents. Originally prepared for a public television series on the presidents, the site is now managed by the University of Virginia.

★ **American Presidents: Life Portraits**

http://www.americanpresidents.org/presidents/president.asp?PresidentNumber=40

A companion site to C-SPAN's 20th anniversary television series, *American Presidents: Life Portraits*, this includes links to many video clips, interviews, and much more.

★ **Internet Public Library, Presidents of the United States (IPL POTUS)**

http://www.ipl.org/div/potus/ghwbush.html

Includes concise information about Bush and his presidency, including links to other Web sites.

★ **George Bush Presidential Library and Museum**

http://bushlibrary.tamu.edu/

This site provides a wealth of information, including text of Bush's presidential speeches and papers, a tour of the museum, many photographs, and related links.

★ **The White House**

http://www.whitehouse.gov/history/presidents/gb41.html

Brief biographical articles on George and Barbara Bush, as well as on each president and first lady.

★ **George Bush's Military Service**

http://www.history.navy.mil/faqs/faq10-1.htm

This navy site provides details about Bush's service during World War II.

Table of Presidents

	1. George Washington	2. John Adams	3. Thomas Jefferson	4. James Madison
Took office	Apr 30 1789	Mar 4 1797	Mar 4 1801	Mar 4 1809
Left office	Mar 3 1797	Mar 3 1801	Mar 3 1809	Mar 3 1817
Birthplace	Westmoreland Co, VA	Braintree, MA	Shadwell, VA	Port Conway, VA
Birth date	Feb 22 1732	Oct 20 1735	Apr 13 1743	Mar 16 1751
Death date	Dec 14 1799	July 4 1826	July 4 1826	June 28 1836

	9. William H. Harrison	10. John Tyler	11. James K. Polk	12. Zachary Taylor
Took office	Mar 4 1841	Apr 6 1841	Mar 4 1845	Mar 5 1849
Left office	**Apr 4 1841•**	Mar 3 1845	Mar 3 1849	**July 9 1850•**
Birthplace	Berkeley, VA	Greenway, VA	Mecklenburg Co, NC	Barboursville, VA
Birth date	Feb 9 1773	Mar 29 1790	Nov 2 1795	Nov 24 1784
Death date	Apr 4 1841	Jan 18 1862	June 15 1849	July 9 1850

	17. Andrew Johnson	18. Ulysses S. Grant	19. Rutherford B. Hayes	20. James A. Garfield
Took office	Apr 15 1865	Mar 4 1869	Mar 5 1877	Mar 4 1881
Left office	Mar 3 1869	Mar 3 1877	Mar 3 1881	**Sept 19 1881•**
Birthplace	Raleigh, NC	Point Pleasant, OH	Delaware, OH	Orange, OH
Birth date	Dec 29 1808	Apr 27 1822	Oct 4 1822	Nov 19 1831
Death date	July 31 1875	July 23 1885	Jan 17 1893	Sept 19 1881

5. James Monroe

Mar 4 1817

Mar 3 1825

Westmoreland Co, VA

Apr 28 1758

July 4 1831

6. John Quincy Adams

Mar 4 1825

Mar 3 1829

Braintree, MA

July 11 1767

Feb 23 1848

7. Andrew Jackson

Mar 4 1829

Mar 3 1837

The Waxhaws, SC

Mar 15 1767

June 8 1845

8. Martin Van Buren

Mar 4 1837

Mar 3 1841

Kinderhook, NY

Dec 5 1782

July 24 1862

13. Millard Fillmore

July 9 1850

Mar 3 1853

Locke Township, NY

Jan 7 1800

Mar 8 1874

14. Franklin Pierce

Mar 4 1853

Mar 3 1857

Hillsborough, NH

Nov 23 1804

Oct 8 1869

15. James Buchanan

Mar 4 1857

Mar 3 1861

Cove Gap, PA

Apr 23 1791

June 1 1868

16. Abraham Lincoln

Mar 4 1861

Apr 15 1865•

Hardin Co, KY

Feb 12 1809

Apr 15 1865

21. Chester A. Arthur

Sept 19 1881

Mar 3 1885

Fairfield, VT

Oct 5 1829

Nov 18 1886

22. Grover Cleveland

Mar 4 1885

Mar 3 1889

Caldwell, NJ

Mar 18 1837

June 24 1908

23. Benjamin Harrison

Mar 4 1889

Mar 3 1893

North Bend, OH

Aug 20 1833

Mar 13 1901

24. Grover Cleveland

Mar 4 1893

Mar 3 1897

Caldwell, NJ

Mar 18 1837

June 24 1908

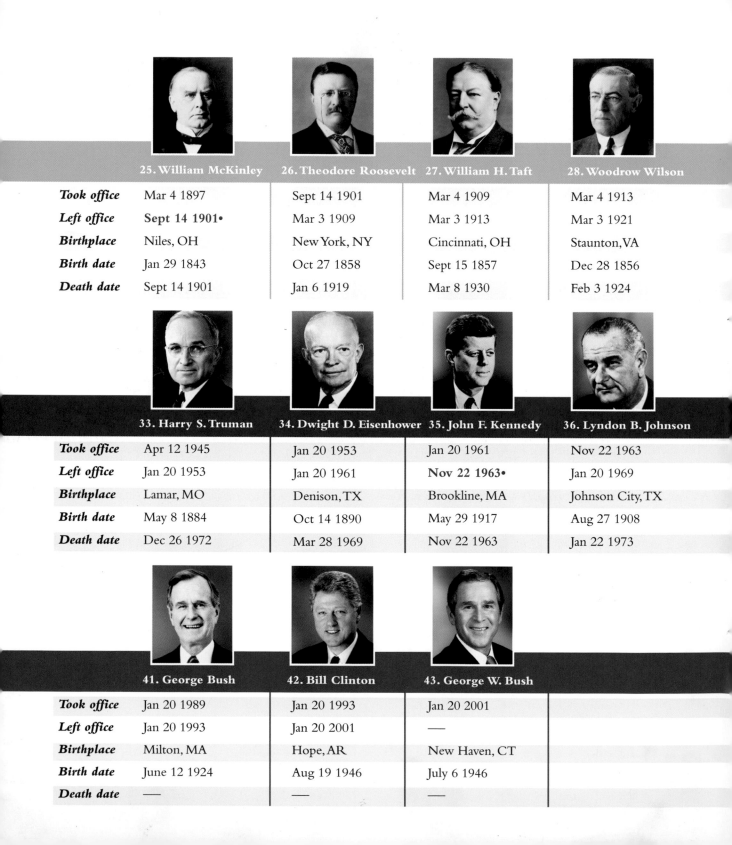

	25. William McKinley	**26. Theodore Roosevelt**	**27. William H. Taft**	**28. Woodrow Wilson**
Took office	Mar 4 1897	Sept 14 1901	Mar 4 1909	Mar 4 1913
Left office	**Sept 14 1901•**	Mar 3 1909	Mar 3 1913	Mar 3 1921
Birthplace	Niles, OH	New York, NY	Cincinnati, OH	Staunton, VA
Birth date	Jan 29 1843	Oct 27 1858	Sept 15 1857	Dec 28 1856
Death date	Sept 14 1901	Jan 6 1919	Mar 8 1930	Feb 3 1924

	33. Harry S. Truman	**34. Dwight D. Eisenhower**	**35. John F. Kennedy**	**36. Lyndon B. Johnson**
Took office	Apr 12 1945	Jan 20 1953	Jan 20 1961	Nov 22 1963
Left office	Jan 20 1953	Jan 20 1961	**Nov 22 1963•**	Jan 20 1969
Birthplace	Lamar, MO	Denison, TX	Brookline, MA	Johnson City, TX
Birth date	May 8 1884	Oct 14 1890	May 29 1917	Aug 27 1908
Death date	Dec 26 1972	Mar 28 1969	Nov 22 1963	Jan 22 1973

	41. George Bush	**42. Bill Clinton**	**43. George W. Bush**	
Took office	Jan 20 1989	Jan 20 1993	Jan 20 2001	
Left office	Jan 20 1993	Jan 20 2001	—	
Birthplace	Milton, MA	Hope, AR	New Haven, CT	
Birth date	June 12 1924	Aug 19 1946	July 6 1946	
Death date	—	—	—	

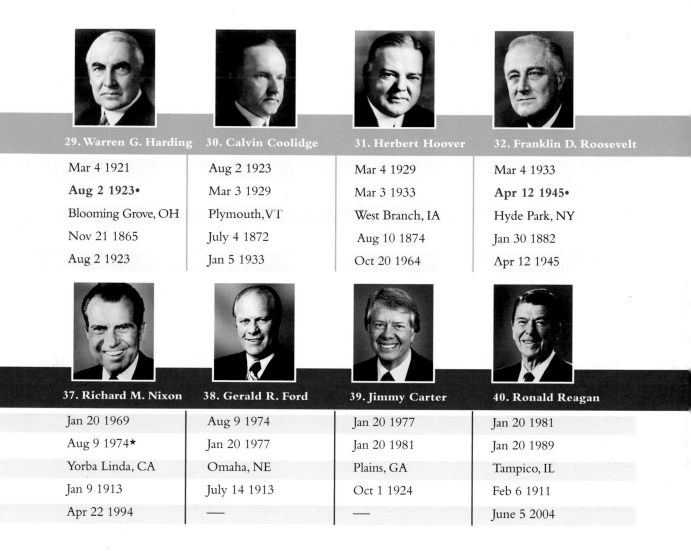

29. Warren G. Harding	30. Calvin Coolidge	31. Herbert Hoover	32. Franklin D. Roosevelt
Mar 4 1921	Aug 2 1923	Mar 4 1929	Mar 4 1933
Aug 2 1923•	Mar 3 1929	Mar 3 1933	**Apr 12 1945•**
Blooming Grove, OH	Plymouth, VT	West Branch, IA	Hyde Park, NY
Nov 21 1865	July 4 1872	Aug 10 1874	Jan 30 1882
Aug 2 1923	Jan 5 1933	Oct 20 1964	Apr 12 1945

37. Richard M. Nixon	38. Gerald R. Ford	39. Jimmy Carter	40. Ronald Reagan
Jan 20 1969	Aug 9 1974	Jan 20 1977	Jan 20 1981
Aug 9 1974★	Jan 20 1977	Jan 20 1981	Jan 20 1989
Yorba Linda, CA	Omaha, NE	Plains, GA	Tampico, IL
Jan 9 1913	July 14 1913	Oct 1 1924	Feb 6 1911
Apr 22 1994	—	—	June 5 2004

• Indicates the president died while in office.
★ Richard Nixon resigned before his term expired.

Index

About the Author

Betsy Ochester is the author of several history books for young readers, including three previous Encyclopedia of Presidents books, *John Tyler*, *Grover Cleveland*, and *Richard Nixon*. In addition, she has published nine titles in two Highlights for Children's series, Which Way USA? and Top Secret Adventures, as well as dozens of puzzles, stories, and articles for young readers. Ms. Ochester is a graduate of Cornell University. After living in Boston, Chicago, and New York City, she now resides in Pittsburgh.